User Experience Microinteractions:

Elevate your user experience with microinteractions.

First Edition

Wayne Hewitt

User Experience Microinteractions:
Elevate your user experience with microinteractions.

Copyright © 2023. All rights reserved by Wayne Hewitt. No part of this book may be reproduced or utilized in any form or by any means, electronic or mechanical, without the express written permission of the publisher. Brief quotations may be used in book reviews.

Printed in the United Kingdom

First Printing, 2023

By the same author

User Experience Design With AI

UX for XR

For Luba, Tanya, and Quinton

Contents

About this book viii

Acknowledgments x

Preface xi

Who Should Read This Book xiii

Chapter 1: Introduction to Microinteractions 1

    Definition of microinteractions. 2

    Importance of microinteractions in UX design 6

    Examples of microinteractions in everyday digital products. 8

Chapter 2: Designing microinteractions. 11

    The process of designing microinteractions. 12

    Best practices for creating effective microinteractions. 15

    Tools and resources for designing microinteractions 18

Chapter 3: microinteractions in Navigation. 20

    How microinteractions can enhance navigation in digital products. 21

    Examples of microinteractions in navigation design. 24

    Best practices for designing microinteractions in navigation. 27

Chapter 4: microinteractions in Feedback. 30

    The role of microinteractions in providing feedback to users. 31

    Examples of microinteractions used for feedback in digital products. 33

    Best practices for designing microinteractions for feedback 35

Chapter 5: microinteractions in Forms. 38

    The role of microinteractions in forms and data input 39

    Examples of microinteractions used in forms. 41

Best practices for designing microinteractions in forms. 43
Chapter 6: microinteractions in Content. 45
    The role of microinteractions in enhancing the presentation of content. 46
    Examples of microinteractions used in content design. 48
    Best practices for designing microinteractions for content. 50
Chapter 7: microinteractions in E-commerce. 52
    How microinteractions can enhance the user experience in e-commerce websites and apps. 53
    Examples of microinteractions used in e-commerce design. 56
    Best practices for designing microinteractions in e-commerce. . 59
Chapter 8: microinteractions in Mobile. 62
    Unique considerations for designing microinteractions in mobile apps. 63
    Examples of microinteractions used in mobile design. 65
    Best practices for designing microinteractions for mobile devices. 68
Chapter 9: microinteractions in Virtual Reality. 71
    The role of microinteractions in virtual reality experiences. 72
    Examples of microinteractions used in VR design. 75
Chapter 10: Conclusion. 78
    The future of microinteractions in UX design. 79
    The importance of testing and iterating microinteractions. 82
    Resources for further learning and staying up-to-date on microinteractions in UX design. 85
    Popular podcasts that cover topics related to user experience (UX) design: 87
    Epilogue 89
    About The Author 91

About this book

"UX Microinteractions" is a comprehensive guide to the world of microinteractions and how they can be used to improve the user experience of digital products. Written by experts in the field of user experience design, this book provides a detailed overview of the key concepts and best practices in microinteractions design.

The book begins by introducing the topic of microinteractions and explaining why they are important for user experience design. Microinteractions are small, subtle interactions that users have with digital products and are often overlooked, yet they play a crucial role in the overall user experience. The book explains that microinteractions can be found in a wide range of products and contexts, from mobile apps and websites to smart devices and even everyday objects.

The book then goes on to explore examples of microinteractions in different contexts, such as mobile apps, websites, and smart devices. It provides a detailed analysis of the best practices for designing effective microinteractions, including how to provide feedback, guide users through a process, and create a sense of delight and engagement. It also explores how microinteractions can be used to create a sense of personality and brand identity for a product.

The book also includes case studies and real-world examples that illustrate the concepts and best practices discussed in the book. These examples provide readers with a deeper understanding of how microinteractions can be used to improve the user experience and help them create more engaging and intuitive user experiences for their own products.

Overall, "UX Microinteractions" is an essential resource for anyone interested in user experience design, specifically in the realm of microinteractions. It provides a solid foundation in the principles and practices of microinteractions design and helps readers create more intuitive and engaging user experiences for their users. With this book, you will learn how to design microinteractions that are functional, useful and delightful, making your product stand out and providing a great user experience.

Acknowledgments

I we would like to express our gratitude to the many people who have helped us along the way.

First and foremost, we would like to thank my family for their unwavering support and encouragement throughout the writing process. Their love and understanding has been invaluable and forever grateful.

We would also like to thank our colleagues and peers in the UX design community who have shared their knowledge and experiences with us. Their insights and perspectives have greatly contributed to the content of this book.

A special thanks to Luba and Tanya, who have provided invaluable research support for this book. Their hard work and dedication have been instrumental in shaping the content and ensuring the quality of the book.

Finally, we would like to thank our readers for taking the time to read this book. We hope that it serves as a valuable resource for anyone interested in micro interactions design and helps them create more engaging and intuitive user experiences.

Preface

In the Preface of our book, "UX Microinteractions," we introduce the topic of microinteractions and explain why they are important for user experience design. Microinteractions are small, subtle interactions that users have with digital products and are often overlooked, yet they play a crucial role in the overall user experience. They can be found in a wide range of products and contexts, from mobile apps and websites to smart devices and even everyday objects.

We begin by explaining that microinteractions are all around us, and that they can make or break the user experience. They are the small animations, sounds, and visual cues that provide users with feedback, guide them through a process, and create a sense of delight and engagement. They can be as simple as a button that changes colour when clicked, or as complex as an animation that guides users through a process.

We then go on to explain that while microinteractions may seem small, they are incredibly powerful in shaping how users perceive and interact with our products. They can be used to guide users through a process, provide feedback, and create a sense of delight and engagement. They can also be used to create a sense of personality and brand identity for a product.

We also explain that despite their importance, many designers and developers overlook microinteractions, often focusing on bigger features and functionality. However, paying attention to the details of microinteractions can make a big difference in how users perceive and interact with our products.

In this book, we aim to provide a comprehensive overview of the key concepts and best practices in microinteractions design. We will explore examples of microinteractions in different contexts, such as mobile apps, websites, and smart devices, and discuss the best practices for designing effective microinteractions. Our goal is to provide our readers with a solid foundation in the principles and practices of microinteractions design and to help them create more intuitive and engaging user experiences.

We hope that this book serves as a valuable resource for our readers and that they will use the knowledge and insights gained to create more intuitive and engaging user experiences for their users.

Who Should Read This Book

UX Microinteractions is an ideal resource for anyone interested in user experience design, specifically in the realm of micro interactions. This book is suitable for designers, developers, and anyone else who wants to understand how micro interactions can be used to improve the user experience of digital products.

Some of the specific audiences who might find this book valuable include:

- UX designers looking to improve their understanding of micro interactions and how to design effective micro interactions for digital products.

- UI designers looking to incorporate micro interactions into their designs to create more engaging and intuitive user experiences.

- Product managers and developers who want to understand the importance of micro interactions in the overall user experience and how to design effective micro interactions for their products.

- Entrepreneurs and start-up founders who want to understand how micro interactions can be used to create a sense of personality and brand identity for their products.

Additionally, students and researchers studying human-computer interaction, user experience design, and related fields may also find this book useful as a resource to gain a better understanding of micro interactions and how they can be used to improve the user experience.

Chapter 1: Introduction to Microinteractions.

Definition of microinteractions.

"Microinteractions" is a term used to describe small, subtle interactions that take place within a digital product or interface. They are often overlooked, yet play a crucial role in enhancing the overall user experience (UX). In this chapter, we'll take a closer look at what microinteractions are, why they are important, and examples of how they are used in everyday digital products.

To start, let's define what we mean by "microinteractions". These are interactions that take place within a digital product or interface that are small in scale, but have a big impact on the user experience. They can be as simple as a button that changes colour when pressed, or as complex as a multi-step animation that guides a user through a task. Essentially, microinteractions are the small details that make a digital product feel more polished, intuitive, and engaging.

So why are microinteractions important? For starters, they add a sense of polish and professionalism to a digital product. By paying attention to the small details and adding microinteractions, a product can feel more polished and professional. Additionally, microinteractions can make a digital product feel more intuitive and easy to use. For example, a button that changes colour when pressed can provide instant feedback to a user, indicating that their action has been recognized. This helps to reduce confusion and frustration, which can be especially important for novice users.

Another key benefit of microinteractions is that they can make a digital product feel more engaging and interactive. For example, a simple animation that plays when a user swipes through a set of images can add a sense of playfulness and engagement to the experience. Similarly, subtle animations that respond to a user's actions can help to create a sense of connection and interaction with the product.

Now, let's take a look at some examples of microinteractions in everyday digital products. One of the most common examples is the "like" button on social media platforms. When a user clicks the button, it changes colour and the number of likes updates, providing instant feedback to the user and indicating that their action has been recognized. Another common example is the "pull to refresh" gesture found in many mobile apps. When a user pulls down on the screen, an animation plays, indicating that the app is refreshing the content. This micro interaction provides feedback to the user, letting them know that their action has been recognized and that new content is on the way.

Another example of microinteractions can be found in e-commerce websites and apps. For example, when a user adds an item to their shopping cart, a small animation might play, indicating that the item has been added. Additionally, the number of items in the cart might update, providing instant feedback to the user. This type of micro interaction can help to create a sense of engagement and interaction with the product, making the experience more enjoyable and satisfying for the user.

Another example of microinteractions can be found in forms, when a user starts to type in an input field, a small label might slide out of the way, making more room for the user to type. This micro interaction can be very useful in forms, as it can make the experience more intuitive and user-friendly, and also it can help users to understand which field they are currently typing into.

Microinteractions are small, subtle interactions that take place within a digital product or interface. They are often overlooked, yet play a crucial role in enhancing the overall user experience.

Microinteractions can make a digital product feel more polished, intuitive, and engaging, and they can also provide feedback to the user, indicating that their action has been recognized. By paying attention to the small details and adding microinteractions, a product can be transformed from a functional tool into an enjoyable and satisfying experience for the user.

It's also worth noting that microinteractions can also be used to convey information or status updates to the user. For example, a small icon or animation that appears when a message has been sent or received can help to keep the user informed and engaged. Similarly, microinteractions can be used to indicate when a download is in progress, or when a task has been completed. This type of feedback can be especially important in situations where the user may be waiting for a response or outcome.

Another important aspect of microinteractions is that they can be used to help guide the user through a task or process. For example, a series of animations or visual cues can be used to guide a user through a multi-step process, such as setting up a new account or making a purchase. This type of guidance can be especially important for novice users, as it can help to reduce confusion and frustration.

It's also worth noting that microinteractions can be used to add a sense of personality and character to a digital product. For example, a playful animation or sound effect can be used to add a sense of humour or quirkiness to an app or website. Similarly, microinteractions can be used to convey a sense of brand identity or style. For example, a high-end fashion website might use subtle animations and visual cues to convey a sense of luxury and elegance.

Microinteractions are small, subtle interactions that play a crucial role in enhancing the overall user experience. They can make a digital product feel more polished, intuitive, and engaging, provide feedback to the user, and guide the user through a task or process. They can also convey information, status updates, personality and brand identity. By paying attention to the small details and adding microinteractions, a digital product can be transformed from a functional tool into an enjoyable and satisfying experience for the user.

Importance of microinteractions in UX design.

In today's digital age, user experience (UX) design is more important than ever. As technology advances and the number of digital products on the market increases, it's crucial for designers to create products that are not only functional but also easy and enjoyable to use. One key element of achieving this is through the use of microinteractions.

Microinteractions are small, subtle interactions that take place within a digital product. These interactions can be as simple as a button that changes colour when pressed, or as complex as a series of animations that happen when a user completes a certain action. They are often used to provide feedback, guide the user, or simply add a touch of delight to the user experience.

The importance of microinteractions in UX design lies in their ability to improve the overall user experience. By providing clear feedback, microinteractions help to guide the user through the product and make it clear what actions can be taken. They also add an element of delight, making the product more enjoyable to use. This is particularly important for mobile apps, which are often used on the go and need to be simple and easy to use.

Microinteractions also play a crucial role in building trust with the user. By providing clear feedback and guiding the user through the product, microinteractions help to build a sense of reliability and dependability. This is particularly important for products that handle sensitive information or require the user to make important decisions.

Another important aspect of microinteractions is that they can help to make the product more efficient. By providing clear feedback and guiding the user, microinteractions can help to reduce the number of steps required to complete a task. This can be particularly important for products that are used frequently, such as mobile apps, where users expect a quick and seamless experience.

Finally, microinteractions can be used to create a sense of brand personality. By using a consistent set of microinteractions throughout the product, designers can create a sense of familiarity and consistency that helps to build a strong brand identity.

Microinteractions play a crucial role in UX design. They help to improve the overall user experience by providing clear feedback, guiding the user, and adding an element of delight. They also help to build trust, make the product more efficient, and create a sense of brand personality. As technology advances and the number of digital products on the market increases, it's important for designers to pay attention to the small details, such as microinteractions, in order to create products that are not only functional but also easy and enjoyable to use.

Examples of microinteractions in everyday digital products.

Examples of microinteractions in everyday digital products are all around us, from our smartphones to our laptops and even our smart home devices. These small interactions are often subtle, but they can have a big impact on the overall user experience.

One of the most common examples of microinteractions can be found in our smartphones. When we receive a text message or a phone call, our phone will vibrate or make a sound to alert us. This is a microinteraction, as it is a small action that serves to inform the user of an event or change in the status of the device. Another example can be found in the volume controls on our smartphones. When we adjust the volume, a small icon will appear on the screen, showing the current volume level. This is another microinteraction, as it provides feedback to the user about the current state of the device.

Another example of microinteractions can be found in social media apps. When we scroll through our feeds, the posts will automatically load as we reach the bottom of the page. This is a microinteraction, as it allows the user to seamlessly continue browsing without having to manually refresh the page. Additionally, when we like or comment on a post, the number of likes or comments will update in real-time, providing immediate feedback to the user about their actions.

In e-commerce websites, microinteractions can be found in various forms. For example, when we add an item to our shopping cart, a small animation will appear to confirm that the item has been added. This is a microinteraction, as it provides feedback to the user and makes the process of adding items to the cart more engaging. Another example can be found in the product pages, when we hover

over an image of a product, it will change to show different angles or additional information, allowing the user to interact with the product and get a better understanding of it before making a purchase.

Microinteractions can also be found in our smart home devices. For example, when we speak to our smart speaker, a light will turn on to indicate that it is listening. This is a microinteraction, as it provides feedback to the user and lets them know that their voice commands are being recognized. Another example can be found in our smart thermostats, when we change the temperature, the thermostat will show an animation of a thermometer moving up or down, providing feedback to the user about the current temperature and the change they made.

Another example of microinteractions can be found in mobile apps, specifically in the notifications. When we receive a notification, for example a message, a small icon will appear on the top of the screen, this icon is a microinteraction as it inform the user that they have received a new message and also it can be a call to action to open the message. Additionally, when we swipe to dismiss a notification, the notification will disappear with a small animation, providing immediate feedback to the user about their actions.

In video streaming apps, microinteractions can be found in the playback controls. When we press the pause button, the play icon will change to a pause icon, this is a microinteraction that provides feedback to the user and let them know the current status of the video. Additionally, when we fast forward or rewind a video, the video will show a small animation, providing feedback to the user about the speed of the video and the changes they made.

In gaming apps, microinteractions can be found in the score, achievements, and rewards. For example, when we score a goal in a football game, a small animation will appear, showing the goal and the score, this is a microinteraction that provides feedback to the user and make the process of scoring a goal more engaging. Additionally, when we unlock an achievement, a small animation will appear, showing the achievement and the rewards, providing feedback to the user about their progress and the rewards they have unlocked.

In virtual reality apps, microinteractions can be found in the interactions with the virtual environment. For example, when we move our hand in front of a virtual object, the object will react with a small animation, this is a microinteraction that provides feedback to the user and make the interaction with the virtual environment more engaging. Additionally, when we move our head around, the virtual environment will change accordingly, providing feedback to the user about their actions.

Microinteractions are found in a wide range of digital products and can be used in many different ways to improve the overall user experience. From providing feedback and informing the user of changes in the status of the device, to making the user experience more engaging and satisfying. It's important to consider microinteractions when designing digital products as they can have a big impact on the overall usability and satisfaction of the users.

Chapter 2: Designing microinteractions.

The process of designing microinteractions.

The process of designing microinteractions is an essential part of the user experience (UX) design process. It involves creating small, subtle interactions within a digital product that enhance the overall user experience. These interactions can be as simple as a button hover state or as complex as a multi-step process, such as setting up a new account.

The first step in designing microinteractions is to identify the user's needs and goals. This involves conducting user research to understand the user's pain points, habits, and preferences. This research can take the form of interviews, surveys, or usability testing. Once the user's needs and goals are understood, the designer can then begin to brainstorm ideas for microinteractions that will meet those needs.

Next, the designer will create a wireframe or prototype of the microinteraction. This will involve creating a basic layout and design for the interaction and testing it with a small group of users. This allows the designer to gather feedback on the design and make any necessary adjustments.

Once the wireframe or prototype is finalized, the designer will then begin to create the final design. This will involve creating high-fidelity mock-ups, animations, and interactions. The designer will also consider the technical feasibility of the design and ensure that it can be implemented within the constraints of the product.

Throughout the design process, it is essential to test the microinteraction with a wider group of users. This can involve conducting usability testing, A/B testing, or other forms of user research. The feedback gathered from these tests can be used to make further adjustments to the design and ensure that it meets the user's needs and goals.

It's also essential to consider the context of the microinteraction. For example, if the microinteraction is being implemented in a mobile app, the designer will need to consider the unique constraints of mobile design, such as screen size and touch-based interactions. Similarly, if the microinteraction is being implemented in a virtual reality experience, the designer will need to consider the unique aspects of VR design, such as the user's point of view and motion-based interactions.

After the final design is complete, it's essential to evaluate the microinteraction's performance, and make changes to improve it. This can involve gathering data on how the microinteraction is being used, such as how often it's being used, how long it takes for users to complete the interaction, and what the success rate is.

This data can be used to understand how well the microinteraction is meeting the user's needs and goals, and identify any areas that need improvement. If a problem is identified, the designer can then make changes to the design, such as simplifying the interaction, or providing more guidance to the user.

It's also important to keep in mind that microinteractions should be consistent with the overall design of the product. This means that they should use the same visual language, styles, and interactions as the rest of the product. Consistency helps to create a cohesive and intuitive user experience.

Another important aspect of designing microinteractions is to consider accessibility. This means that the microinteraction should be usable by people with disabilities, such as those who are blind or have low vision. This can involve providing alternative text for images, or ensuring that the interaction can be completed using a keyboard.

Lastly, it's essential to stay up-to-date with the latest trends and best practices in microinteraction design. This can involve staying informed about the latest design tools and technologies, reading articles and blogs about microinteraction design, and following other designers on social media.

Designing microinteractions is a critical aspect of creating a successful user experience. It's essential to conduct user research, create wireframes and prototypes, test with users, and gather data to evaluate the performance of the microinteraction. By following these best practices, designers can create microinteractions that enhance the overall user experience, are consistent with the product's design and are accessible to all users.

Best practices for creating effective microinteractions.

When it comes to designing microinteractions, there are certain best practices that can help ensure that they are effective and enhance the overall user experience. Here are a few key things to keep in mind when creating microinteractions:

1. Make them purposeful: Microinteractions should serve a specific purpose and add value to the user experience. Before designing a micro interaction, ask yourself what problem you are trying to solve and how this interaction will help the user.

2. Keep them simple: Microinteractions should be easy to understand and use. Avoid adding unnecessary elements or complexity to the design. The simpler the interaction, the more likely it is to be understood and used correctly by the user.

3. Make them consistent: Microinteractions should be consistent with the overall design and branding of the product. This will help create a sense of familiarity and ease of use for the user.

4. Make them discoverable: Microinteractions should be easy to find and understand. Make sure that the user knows what to expect when interacting with the element and what will happen as a result.

5. Make them feedback: Microinteractions should provide feedback to the user, letting them know that the interaction has taken place and what the outcome was. This can be done through visual, auditory, or haptic cues.

6. Make them accessible: Microinteractions should be designed with accessibility in mind, so that they can be used by as many people as possible. This includes designing for users with visual, auditory, or motor impairments.

7. Test and iterate: As with any design, it's important to test microinteractions with real users and gather feedback. Use this feedback to iterate and improve the design.

By keeping these best practices in mind, you can create microinteractions that are effective and add value to the user experience.

It's important to keep in mind that Microinteractions are small but mighty, and the design of them should be done with care. The little details matter and can make or break the user experience. The purpose of microinteractions is to simplify complex processes and make them more human and intuitive. They are the glue that holds together the user interface, and it is essential that they are designed correctly.

When designing microinteractions, it is crucial to make them consistent with the overall design and branding of the product. This helps create a sense of familiarity and ease of use for the user. When a user interacts with an element, they should know what to expect and what will happen as a result. It's also essential to make them discoverable, so the user knows what they are interacting with and what the outcome will be.

Microinteractions also need to be accessible. It is essential that they can be used by as many people as possible, regardless of their abilities. This includes designing for users with visual, auditory, or motor impairments.

It's also vital to test and iterate. As with any design, it's important to test microinteractions with real users and gather feedback. Use this feedback to iterate and improve the design. This is the best way to ensure that the microinteractions are effective and add value to the user experience.

Microinteractions are a crucial aspect of user experience design. They simplify complex processes, make them more human and intuitive, and glue together the user interface. Designing microinteractions can be tricky, but by keeping best practices in mind such as making them purposeful, simple, consistent, discoverable, feedback, accessible, and testing and iterating, you can create microinteractions that are effective and enhance the overall user experience.

Tools and resources for designing microinteractions.

When it comes to designing microinteractions, there are a variety of tools and resources available to help you create effective and engaging designs. In this chapter, we'll take a look at some of the most popular and useful tools for designing microinteractions, as well as some resources for learning more about this area of UX design.

One of the most important tools for designing microinteractions is a wireframing and prototyping tool. These tools allow you to create rough sketches of your microinteractions, as well as test them out with users. Popular wireframing and prototyping tools include Sketch, Figma, and InVision. These tools are easy to use and have a wide range of pre-built UI elements and interactions, which makes it easy to create microinteractions.

Another useful tool for designing microinteractions is animation software. This allows you to create animations for your microinteractions, which can help make them more engaging and easy to understand. Popular animation software includes After Effects and Adobe XD. These tools are great for creating animations that are smooth and polished, and can be exported as GIFs or video files to be used in your wireframes or prototypes.

For designers who are looking for inspiration, there are a number of resources available, such as Dribble and Behance. These platforms showcase work from other designers and can provide inspiration for your own microinteractions. Additionally, there are a number of blogs and podcasts that focus on microinteractions and UX design, such as UX Design and UX Collective. These resources can provide valuable insights and inspiration for your work.

When it comes to testing your microinteractions, it's important to have a user testing tool. These tools allow you to get feedback from real users on your microinteractions, which can help you improve your designs. Popular user testing tools include User Testing and Optimal Workshop. These tools are great for getting feedback on your microinteractions, as well as learning more about user behaviour and preferences.

Finally, there are a number of resources available for learning more about microinteractions and UX design. One of the best ways to learn is by taking online courses. There are a number of online courses available on microinteractions and UX design, such as those offered by Udemy and Coursera. These courses can provide a great introduction to the topic, and can help you learn more about best practices and tools for designing microinteractions.

Designing microinteractions is an important aspect of user experience design. There are a variety of tools and resources available that can help you create effective and engaging microinteractions, including wireframing and prototyping tools, animation software, design inspiration resources, user testing tools, and online courses. By using these tools and resources, you can improve your microinteractions and create a better user experience for your digital products.

Chapter 3: microinteractions in Navigation.

How microinteractions can enhance navigation in digital products.

In today's digital landscape, navigation is a crucial aspect of user experience (UX) design. Navigation allows users to move seamlessly through a digital product, find the information they need, and complete tasks efficiently. Microinteractions play a significant role in enhancing navigation in digital products. In this chapter, we will explore how microinteractions can improve navigation, provide examples of microinteractions used in navigation design, and discuss best practices for designing microinteractions in navigation.

Microinteractions are small interactions that occur within a digital product, such as a button hover or a pull-to-refresh gesture. They can be used to provide feedback, guide the user, and create delightful moments within a product. In navigation, microinteractions can be used to make the navigation more intuitive, efficient, and engaging.

One way microinteractions can enhance navigation is by providing clear feedback to the user. For example, when a user hovers over a navigation item, a micro interaction can be used to highlight the selected item and give the user a preview of the destination page. This can help the user understand where they are in the product, and where they can go next. Microinteractions can also be used to provide feedback when a user performs an action, such as a pull-to-refresh gesture. For example, when a user pulls down on a page, a micro interaction can be used to indicate that the page is refreshing. This can help the user understand that their action has been recognized and that the page is loading new content.

Another way microinteractions can enhance navigation is by guiding the user. For example, when a user clicks on a navigation item, a microinteraction can be used to animate the transition to the next page. This can help the user understand where they are in the product, and where they can go next. Microinteractions can also be used to guide the user through a task, such as a step-by-step process. For example, when a user clicks on a navigation item, a micro interaction can be used to animate the transition to the next page. This can help the user understand where they are in the process and what they need to do next.

Lastly, microinteractions can enhance navigation by creating delightful moments within a product. For example, when a user completes a task, a micro interaction can be used to celebrate the accomplishment. This can be in form of small animation, a sound, or a message. These small moments of delight can help create a positive and memorable user experience.

In terms of examples, we can see microinteractions in navigation in many digital products such as websites, mobile apps, and software. One example is the navigation menu on a website. When a user hovers over a navigation item, a micro interaction can be used to highlight the selected item and give the user a preview of the destination page. Another example is the pull-to-refresh gesture on a mobile app. When a user pulls down on a page, a micro interaction can be used to indicate that the page is refreshing.

When it comes to best practices for designing microinteractions in navigation, it is important to keep in mind that microinteractions should be simple, intuitive, and consistent. It's important to design microinteractions that are in line with the overall design and brand of the product. They should be easy to understand and use without any explicit instructions. Microinteractions should also be consistent throughout the product, so the user knows what to expect. Finally, it is important to test microinteractions with users to ensure they are intuitive and efficient.

Microinteractions play a crucial role in enhancing navigation in digital products. They can be used to provide clear feedback, guide the user, and create delightful moments within a product. By designing microinteractions that are simple , intuitive, and consistent, designers can create a seamless and enjoyable user experience. Additionally, by testing microinteractions with users, designers can ensure that they are easy to understand and use, and that they serve their intended purpose effectively.

It's also important to remember that microinteractions should be used in moderation, and not overused. Too many microinteractions can be overwhelming and can actually detract from the user experience. Instead, designers should focus on using microinteractions in strategic places, such as key navigation areas, to enhance the overall user experience.

Microinteractions can greatly enhance navigation in digital products by providing clear feedback, guiding the user, and creating delightful moments within a product. Designers should focus on creating simple, intuitive, and consistent microinteractions, and should test them with users to ensure they are effective. By using microinteractions in a strategic and moderate way, designers can create an enjoyable and seamless user experience.

Examples of microinteractions in navigation design.

Microinteractions in navigation design refer to the small, subtle animations or interactions that are used to guide users through a digital product. These interactions can be used to help users understand where they are in the product, what options are available to them, and how to access different parts of the product. In this chapter, we will explore some examples of microinteractions in navigation design, and how they can be used to enhance the user experience.

One of the most common examples of microinteractions in navigation design is the use of hover states. When a user hovers over a navigation link or button, a small animation or change in appearance can be used to indicate that the item is clickable. This can be as simple as a change in colour, or a subtle movement of the button. This type of interaction gives users a visual cue that they can interact with an element, without having to click on it, making it more discoverable.

Another example of microinteractions in navigation design is the use of sliding menus. These types of menus are often used on mobile devices, where screen real estate is limited. When a user taps on a navigation link, a sliding menu will appear, displaying additional options. This interaction is useful for hiding less important options and keeping the navigation simple and easy to use.

Another example of microinteractions in navigation design is the use of tooltips. These are small pop-up messages that appear when a user hovers over a specific element. Tooltips can be used to provide additional information about a navigation link or button, such as where it will take the user, or what actions they can take. This type of interaction is useful for providing users with more context, without cluttering the navigation.

Microinteractions can also be used to create a sense of hierarchy in navigation. For example, using different colours or sizes of buttons to indicate the importance of different navigation links. This can help users understand which links are the most important, and where to focus their attention. Additionally, microinteractions can be used to create a sense of progress through a product, such as highlighting the current page or step in a process.

Another example of microinteractions in navigation design is the use of loaders. Loaders are often used when a user is waiting for something to load, such as a new page or content. They can be used to indicate the progress of the load and prevent the user from thinking the app or website is not responding. It also gives a sense of anticipation and keeps the user engaged.

Another example of microinteractions in navigation design is the use of scroll-triggered animations. These types of animations can be used to create a more engaging and dynamic user experience by bringing elements to life as the user scrolls through the product. For example, when a user scrolls to a certain section of a website, an animation can be triggered that causes an image to slide into view or text to appear in a more dynamic way. This can be used to draw the user's attention to important content, or to create a sense of movement and engagement.

Another example of microinteractions in navigation design is the use of "back-to-top" buttons. These buttons are typically placed at the bottom of a website or app, and allow the user to quickly scroll back to the top of the page without having to manually scroll through all the content. These buttons can be designed to be subtle, only appearing when the user scrolls down far enough, or they can be more prominent. This type of micro interaction can be particularly useful for websites or apps with a lot of content, as it can save users time and effort when trying to navigate through the content.

In addition, microinteractions can be used to enhance the search functionality of a digital product. For example, when a user begins typing in a search bar, a list of suggested search results can appear, which can be refined as the user continues to type. This type of micro interaction can help users find what they are looking for more quickly, and can also be used to guide users to relevant content.

Lastly, microinteractions can be used to create a sense of personalization and customization. For example, by allowing users to change the colour scheme or layout of a product, microinteractions can be used to create a more tailored user experience. This can be particularly useful for apps or websites that are used frequently, as it can help users feel more connected to the product and more in control of their experience.

Microinteractions in navigation design can be used in a variety of ways to enhance the user experience. From providing visual cues and creating a sense of hierarchy, to creating a sense of progress and engagement, microinteractions can make digital products more intuitive, engaging, and easy to use. By understanding the different types of microinteractions and how they can be used in navigation design, digital product designers and developers can create more effective and user-friendly products.

Best practices for designing microinteractions in navigation.

When designing microinteractions for navigation, it's important to keep in mind that their main purpose is to guide users through the digital product and make it easy for them to find what they're looking for. Here are some best practices to keep in mind when designing microinteractions for navigation:

1. Keep it simple: Navigation microinteractions should be easy to understand and use, without any unnecessary complexity. They should also be consistent with the overall design and style of the digital product.

2. Make it visible: Navigation microinteractions should be placed in locations where they are easy to find and use, such as the top navigation bar or along the side of the screen. They should also be clearly labelled and explain what they do.

3. Be contextually aware: Navigation microinteractions should be responsive to the user's needs and provide relevant information. For example, if a user is searching for a specific item on an e-commerce website, the microinteraction could display a list of suggested items or a filter option that narrows down the search results.

4. Test and iterate: It's important to test the navigation microinteractions with real users and gather feedback to make sure they are working as intended. Based on that feedback, you can make adjustments and improve the microinteraction.

5. Keep accessibility in mind: Navigation microinteractions should be accessible to as many users as possible, including those with disabilities. This means using clear and simple language, providing alternative ways to interact with the microinteraction (e.g. keyboard shortcuts), and ensuring that the microinteraction can be used with assistive technologies.

6. Provide clear feedback: Navigation microinteractions should provide clear feedback to the user, such as a confirmation message or an animation that indicates the action has been completed.

7. Make it consistent: Navigation microinteractions should be consistent throughout the digital product, in terms of their visual and interaction patterns. This will help users feel more comfortable and familiar with the product, making it easier for them to navigate.

8. Make it fast: Navigation microinteractions should be fast and responsive, so that users don't have to wait long for something to happen. This is particularly important when it comes to searching and filtering.

9. Make it adaptive: Navigation microinteractions should be adaptive, meaning they should change and improve over time based on the user's behavior and preferences.

10. Make it fun: Navigation microinteractions can be made more engaging and fun if done correctly. This can be achieved by using animations, sound effects, or gamification techniques.

By following these best practices, you can create effective and intuitive navigation microinteractions that will improve the overall user experience of your digital product. Remember that testing, iterating and gathering feedback from users is key to improve and adapt the microinteractions.

Chapter 4: microinteractions in Feedback.

The role of microinteractions in providing feedback to users.

Microinteractions are small interactions that take place within a digital product or service, such as a button press or a notification. These interactions are designed to make the user experience more seamless, intuitive, and satisfying. When it comes to feedback, microinteractions play a vital role in communicating the outcome of an action taken by the user.

One of the most important aspects of feedback is that it should be immediate and relevant to the user's action. Microinteractions allow designers to provide this type of feedback by allowing them to design interactions that happen in real-time and are directly related to the user's action. For example, when a user clicks a "like" button on a social media post, a microinteraction can be designed to show a visual cue, such as a heart animation, to indicate that the action was successful. This immediate feedback lets the user know that their action has been registered and confirms that the system is working as expected.

Another important aspect of feedback is that it should be clear and informative. Microinteractions allow designers to provide clear and informative feedback by allowing them to design interactions that are easy to understand. For example, when a user attempts to submit a form with missing information, a microinteraction can be designed to highlight the missing fields and display an error message. This clear and informative feedback lets the user know what they need to do to correct the issue and move forward.

Microinteractions also play a vital role in providing feedback that is engaging and satisfying. These interactions can be designed to be playful and fun, which can help to create a more enjoyable user experience. For example, when a user completes a task, a microinteraction can be designed to show a celebratory animation, such as confetti or balloons. This engaging and satisfying feedback can help to make the user feel accomplished and encourage them to continue using the product or service.

In addition to providing feedback, microinteractions can also be used to guide users through a task. For example, when a user is filling out a form, a microinteraction can be designed to display a tooltip with instructions on how to complete the next field. This guidance can help to make the task less daunting and more manageable for the user.

Microinteractions play a vital role in providing feedback to users. These small interactions allow designers to provide immediate and relevant feedback, clear and informative feedback, engaging and satisfying feedback, and guidance through a task. By using microinteractions, designers can create a more seamless, intuitive, and satisfying user experience. In order to achieve that, designers should always be testing and iterating microinteractions, making sure they are providing the best possible feedback to the users.

Examples of microinteractions used for feedback in digital products.

When it comes to providing feedback to users, microinteractions can play a crucial role in making the experience seamless and intuitive. In this chapter, we will explore some examples of microinteractions used for feedback in digital products, and discuss best practices for designing microinteractions for feedback.

One of the most common examples of microinteractions used for feedback is the "like" button on social media platforms. When a user clicks on the "like" button, the button animates with a subtle pulse and the number of likes increases by one. This gives the user immediate visual feedback that their action has been registered and gives them a sense of engagement with the platform.

Another example of microinteractions used for feedback is the pull-to-refresh gesture on mobile apps. When a user pulls down on the screen, an animation of a spinning wheel or refresh icon is displayed, indicating that the app is loading new content. This gives the user feedback that their action has been registered and they can expect new content to be displayed.

In-app notifications are also a great example of microinteractions used for feedback. When a user receives a notification, a small icon or banner appears on the screen, indicating that there is new information for the user to view. This type of micro interaction not only provides feedback to the user, but it also serves as a reminder to check the app for new content.

Another example of microinteractions used for feedback is the "loading" animation. When a user initiates an action that requires the app to load data, a loading animation is displayed, indicating that the app is working and the user's action has been registered. This type of micro interaction provides feedback to the user that their action is being processed and they can expect the desired outcome soon.

Finally, error messages are a great example of microinteractions used for feedback. When a user input is invalid or the app encounters an error, an error message is displayed, indicating to the user what went wrong. Error messages often include a short description of the problem and a way to fix it, providing immediate feedback and guidance to the user.

When designing microinteractions for feedback, it's important to keep in mind that the goal is to provide instant and intuitive feedback to the user. The animation should be subtle, yet noticeable and it should indicate clearly the result of the user's action. It's also important to consider the context in which the micro interaction will be used, and to make sure that it aligns with the overall design of the app.

Microinteractions play an important role in providing feedback to users in digital products. They can be used to give instant visual feedback, to remind users to check the app, to indicate that an action is being processed, and to provide guidance when there's an error. By designing microinteractions for feedback that are subtle, noticeable, and intuitive, designers can enhance the user experience and make the interaction more seamless.

Best practices for designing microinteractions for feedback.

Best practices for designing microinteractions for feedback involve creating clear, concise, and immediate feedback that is tailored to the user's actions. These microinteractions should be designed to provide users with the information they need to understand how their actions affect the system or application they are using.

First and foremost, it is important to consider the context of the feedback. Feedback should be relevant to the user's current task or action, and should be presented in a way that is easy to understand. This means that feedback should be provided in the user's native language, and should use simple and familiar words and phrases. It is also important to consider the user's level of technical expertise when designing feedback, as more technical users may require more detailed information than non-technical users.

Next, it is important to ensure that feedback is immediate and responsive. Users should receive feedback as soon as they take an action, and the feedback should reflect the result of that action. This helps to prevent confusion and frustration, and allows users to quickly understand how their actions have affected the system or application.

Another key aspect of designing effective feedback microinteractions is to make sure that they are consistent across the application or system. Consistency helps to ensure that users understand how to use the system or application and can easily predict what will happen when they take an action. This can be achieved by using similar design elements, such as colour, iconography, and layout, throughout the application or system.

In addition, microinteractions for feedback should be designed to be as unobtrusive as possible. Users should not feel like they are being constantly interrupted or bombarded with feedback. Feedback should be presented in a way that does not disrupt the user's flow of work, and should be easy to dismiss if it is not needed. This can be achieved by using subtle animations or by displaying feedback in a non-intrusive way, such as a small notification at the bottom of the screen.

It's also important to consider accessibility when designing microinteractions for feedback. Feedback should be provided in a way that is accessible to users with disabilities, such as providing audio feedback for users who are visually impaired. This will ensure that all users can understand the feedback and take appropriate action based on it.

Another aspect to consider when designing microinteractions for feedback is the use of visual cues. Visual cues, such as colours, icons, and animations, can be used to indicate the status of an action or to provide information in a non-verbal way. For example, a green colour can be used to indicate that an action was successful, while a red colour can indicate an error. Icons can be used to indicate the type of feedback being provided, such as a checkmark for success or an exclamation mark for an error. Animations can be used to grab the user's attention and provide feedback in a more engaging way.

It's also important to consider the user's emotional state when providing feedback. Feedback can have a significant impact on a user's emotional state, so it's important to design feedback that is appropriate for the context. For example, if an error occurs, the feedback should be designed to be apologetic and helpful, rather than accusatory. This can be achieved by using a friendly tone and providing suggestions for how to resolve the issue.

Another best practice is to use feedback as an opportunity to guide users. Feedback can be used to guide users through a task or to help them understand how to use a feature. For example, when a user first signs up for an account, feedback can be used to guide them through the process of setting up their profile. This can be achieved by providing step-by-step instructions and highlighting the important elements of the process.

In addition, it's important to consider the user's device when designing feedback microinteractions. The device being used can have a significant impact on the design of feedback microinteractions. For example, feedback on a mobile device should be designed to be easy to read and understand on a small screen, whereas feedback on a desktop computer can be more detailed and complex.

Finally, it's important to keep in mind the overall user experience when designing feedback microinteractions. Feedback microinteractions should be designed to enhance the overall user experience, rather than detract from it. This means that feedback microinteractions should be designed to be as seamless and unobtrusive as possible, and should be integrated into the overall design of the application or system.

Designing effective microinteractions for feedback is a complex task that requires designers to consider a variety of factors, such as context, immediacy, consistency, accessibility, testing, visual cues, emotional state, guidance, device and overall user experience. By following these best practices, designers can create feedback microinteractions that are tailored to the user's needs and provide clear, concise and immediate information that will help users understand how their actions affect the system or application they are using, all while enhancing their overall user experience.

Chapter 5: microinteractions in Forms.

The role of microinteractions in forms and data input.

The role of microinteractions in forms and data input is incredibly important when it comes to providing a smooth and efficient user experience. Forms are often used to collect information from users, whether it be for registration, checkout, or data entry. In order for these forms to be successful, they must be intuitive, easy to use, and provide clear feedback to the user. Microinteractions play a critical role in achieving these goals.

One of the key ways microinteractions can enhance forms is by providing clear feedback to the user. For example, if a user enters an invalid email address, a microinteraction can be used to display an error message that is clear and easy to understand. This can be done through visual cues such as a red border around the input field or an error icon that appears next to the field. Additionally, microinteractions can be used to provide real-time feedback, such as a green checkmark that appears as soon as the user has entered a valid email address.

Microinteractions can also be used to guide the user through the form-filling process. For example, a microinteraction can be used to highlight the next input field as the user completes each field. This not only makes it easier for the user to understand where they are in the form, but it also helps to reduce errors by ensuring the user is focused on the correct field at all times.

Another way microinteractions can enhance forms is by providing an intuitive and easy-to-use experience. For example, a microinteraction can be used to reveal additional input fields only when they are needed. This can help to simplify the form and make it less overwhelming for the user, as they are only presented with the fields they need to fill in. Additionally, microinteractions can be used to provide clear and obvious instructions to the user, such as a tooltip that appears when the user hovers over an input field.

In addition to these examples, microinteractions can also be used to improve the overall aesthetic of a form and make it more visually appealing. For example, microinteractions can be used to create smooth and subtle animations that help to guide the user through the form and make it more engaging.

Microinteractions play a crucial role in enhancing the user experience of forms and data input. They can provide clear feedback, guide the user through the form-filling process, make the form more intuitive and easy to use, and improve the overall aesthetic of the form. By incorporating microinteractions into your form designs, you can help to ensure that your users have a smooth and efficient experience when providing you with their information.

Examples of microinteractions used in forms.

Microinteractions in forms are a crucial aspect of user experience design. They provide users with feedback and guidance as they fill out forms, making the process more efficient and less frustrating. In this chapter, we will take a closer look at some examples of microinteractions used in forms and discuss best practices for designing them.

One of the most common microinteractions used in forms is the error message. When a user enters an incorrect or incomplete piece of information, the form will display an error message to inform the user of the problem. The error message should be clear and easy to understand, and it should be placed close to the field where the error occurred. For example, if a user forgets to enter their email address, the error message might say "Please enter your email address." This is a simple and effective way to guide the user and prevent errors.

Another common micro interaction used in forms is the progress indicator. This is a visual representation of how many fields the user has completed and how many are left. Progress indicators can take many forms, such as a bar that fills up as the user completes more fields, or a series of dots that light up as the user progresses. This micro interaction gives the user a sense of progress and helps to keep them motivated.

Validation is also an important micro interaction used in forms. It happens when the user is entering information and the system is checking if the information is correct or not. This can be done in real time, for example, when the user enters their email address and the system checks if it is in the correct format. Or it can happen when the user submits the form and the system checks all the information before proceeding. This micro interaction helps to prevent errors and improves the overall user experience.

Another example of microinteractions in forms is the autocomplete feature. This feature automatically suggests options based on what the user is typing. This can be particularly useful for fields such as addresses, as it saves the user time and improves the accuracy of the information entered. Autocomplete can also be used for other fields such as names, email addresses, or even search queries.

Finally, microinteractions such as hover effects and animations can also be used in forms to enhance the overall user experience. For example, when a user hover over a field, the field can change colour or an icon can appear, providing a clear indication of the user's intent. Animations can also be used to guide the user's attention or to indicate that a form has been submitted successfully.

Microinteractions in forms play an important role in user experience design. They provide users with feedback, guidance, and validation, making the process of filling out forms more efficient and less frustrating. When designing microinteractions for forms, it is important to keep them simple, clear, and easy to understand. It's also good to keep in mind that microinteractions should be tested and iterated to ensure that they are effective and efficient.

Best practices for designing microinteractions in forms.

Best practices for designing microinteractions in forms are an essential aspect of user experience (UX) design. Microinteractions in forms serve to guide the user through the process of inputting information, providing feedback, and reducing errors. In this chapter, we will discuss some best practices for designing microinteractions in forms that can help improve the overall user experience.

First, it is crucial to understand the user's task and goals when designing microinteractions in forms. Before designing any microinteractions, it is essential to conduct user research to understand the user's needs, pain points, and goals. This information can be used to inform the design of microinteractions that will make the form-filling process as smooth and efficient as possible.

One best practice for designing microinteractions in forms is to provide clear and concise instructions for each field. This can be done by providing clear labels, tooltips, or other forms of guidance to help the user understand what information is required in each field. It is also important to ensure that the instructions are consistent throughout the form to prevent confusion.

Another best practice is to provide real-time validation and feedback as the user is filling out the form. For example, providing instant feedback on whether an email address or password is valid can help the user quickly identify and correct any errors. This can also prevent the user from submitting the form with incorrect information, saving them time and frustration.

It's also important to consider the user's input method when designing microinteractions in forms. For example, if the form is optimized for mobile devices, it should be designed to take into account the smaller screen size and different input methods such as touch. This can be achieved by using larger font sizes, simpler layouts, and larger buttons.

Another best practice is to use progressive disclosure in forms. Progressive disclosure is a technique that involves revealing form fields only when they are needed. This can help to reduce the number of fields that the user needs to fill out, making the form-filling process less overwhelming.

Finally, it is essential to test the microinteractions in forms with real users to ensure they are effective and user-friendly. This can be done through user testing, where the form is presented to a group of users and their interactions and feedback are observed and recorded. This feedback can then be used to iterate and improve the design of the microinteractions.

Designing microinteractions in forms is an essential aspect of UX design. By understanding the user's task and goals, providing clear instructions, real-time validation, and feedback, considering the input method, using progressive disclosure, and testing with real users, designers can create forms that are user-friendly and efficient.

Chapter 6: microinteractions in Content.

The role of microinteractions in enhancing the presentation of content.

In today's digital landscape, users are constantly bombarded with an overwhelming amount of content. To stand out and capture the attention of users, it's important for digital products to not only have high-quality content, but also to present it in an engaging and interactive way. Microinteractions play a crucial role in enhancing the presentation of content and making it more engaging for users.

Microinteractions are small, subtle animations or interactions that are triggered by a user's actions. They can be used to give feedback, guide the user, or add personality to a product. In terms of enhancing the presentation of content, microinteractions can be used in a variety of ways.

One way microinteractions can enhance content presentation is by adding a sense of interactivity. For example, when a user hovers over a thumbnail image on a website, it could enlarge slightly or change colour to indicate that it's clickable. This small interaction makes the content more engaging and interactive for the user. Similarly, microinteractions can be used to reveal more information about a piece of content. A user might click on an image and have it expand to reveal more details or a caption. This helps to make the content more accessible and user-friendly.

Another way microinteractions can enhance content presentation is by providing a sense of context and hierarchy. For example, a website might use microinteractions to highlight the most important pieces of content. When a user scrolls over a certain piece of content, it could animate to draw the user's attention. This helps to guide the user to the most important information and makes it easier to navigate the content. Microinteractions can also be used to indicate the relative importance of different pieces of content. For example, a news website might use microinteractions to indicate which articles are trending or have been recently updated.

Microinteractions can also be used to add personality and character to a digital product. For example, a weather app might use microinteractions to indicate the current weather conditions. Instead of simply displaying the temperature, the app might use microinteractions to animate a sun for a sunny day or raindrops for a rainy day. This helps to make the content more engaging and memorable for users.

In addition to these examples, microinteractions can also be used in other ways to enhance the presentation of content such as providing a sense of progression or providing more engaging multimedia experiences.

Microinteractions play a crucial role in enhancing the presentation of content in digital products. They can be used to add interactivity, provide context and hierarchy, add personality, and guide the user. By incorporating microinteractions into the design, digital products can be made more engaging, memorable and user-friendly. As a designer, it's important to keep in mind the potential of microinteractions and how they can be used to enhance the overall user experience.

Examples of microinteractions used in content design.

Microinteractions in content design refer to the small interactions that occur when a user interacts with the content of a digital product. These interactions can be used to enhance the overall user experience and make the content more engaging and interactive.

One example of a microinteraction used in content design is the "like" button on social media platforms. When a user clicks the "like" button, the button changes colour, and a small notification appears on the screen, indicating that the user's action has been registered. This simple microinteraction provides immediate feedback to the user and also serves as a way for them to interact with the content and express their engagement with it.

Another example is the "read more" button, which is often used on websites and blogs to hide lengthy content behind a button that users can click on to view more. This microinteraction allows users to quickly scan through the content and decide which articles they want to read in more detail. It also helps keep the layout of the page clean and uncluttered.

A third example is the use of hover effects on images in a gallery. When a user hovers their cursor over an image, a small caption or a preview of the image may appear. This microinteraction allows users to quickly preview the content of an image without having to click on it. It also provides a more engaging and interactive experience for the user.

Microinteractions can also be used to enhance the navigation of content. For example, a "table of contents" button can be used to provide a quick and easy way for users to navigate through long-form content. When the user clicks on the button, a list of headings and subheadings appears, allowing them to jump to the section of the content that interests them most.

Another example is the use of pagination to break up long-form content into smaller, more manageable chunks. This microinteraction allows users to navigate through the content in a way that feels more natural and less overwhelming. It also helps keep the layout of the page clean and uncluttered.

In addition, microinteractions can be used to enhance the presentation of content. For example, the use of animations and transitions can make the content feel more dynamic and engaging. For instance, when a user scrolls down a page, the content might fade in gradually, providing a more pleasant and engaging experience.

Finally, microinteractions can be used to enhance the interactive nature of content. For example, quizzes and polls can be used to engage users and encourage them to interact with the content in a more meaningful way. These microinteractions can be used to test the user's knowledge or gather their opinions on a particular topic, making the content more interactive and engaging.

Microinteractions play a crucial role in enhancing the overall user experience of content design. They allow users to interact with the content in a more meaningful way and make the content more engaging and interactive. From "like" button to hover effects, from "read more" button to table of contents, from pagination to animations and transitions, microinteractions are a small but powerful tool for UX designers to take into account when designing digital products.

Best practices for designing microinteractions for content.

Best practices for designing microinteractions for content are essential for creating a seamless and engaging user experience. These small, subtle interactions can enhance the way users interact with and consume content, making it more interactive and meaningful. In this chapter, we will explore some of the best practices for designing microinteractions for content, including how to use them effectively, how to design them, and what types of content they work best with.

First, it's important to understand how and when to use microinteractions for content. Microinteractions should be used to enhance the user experience, not detract from it. They should be subtle and not overwhelming, used only when they add value to the content. For example, a microinteraction that allows users to expand and collapse text or images can be helpful for lengthy articles or guides, but it would not be necessary for a short news article. Additionally, microinteractions should be used consistently throughout the content, rather than sporadically.

When designing microinteractions for content, it's important to keep the user in mind. The goal is to make the content more interactive and engaging, not to distract or confuse the user. This means that microinteractions should be intuitive and easy to use, with clear labels or instructions. They should also be visually consistent with the rest of the content, so as not to disrupt the flow of the user experience.

One of the most important best practices for designing microinteractions for content is to keep it simple. Microinteractions should be minimalistic, avoiding unnecessary complexity. The simpler the microinteraction, the more likely it is to be used and understood by the user.

Another key best practice is to test your microinteractions before launching. User testing is an essential step in the design process, as it allows you to get feedback on the microinteractions and make any necessary adjustments. This will ensure that the microinteractions are intuitive and effective, and that they enhance the user experience, rather than detracting from it.

There are different types of content that microinteractions can be used with, and each type may require a different approach. For example, microinteractions can be used to enhance the reading experience, such as allowing users to change the font size or background color of text. They can also be used to make videos and images more interactive, such as allowing users to zoom in and out or rotate an image. Microinteractions can also be used to make data more interactive, such as allowing users to filter or sort data in a table.

Microinteractions for content can be a powerful tool for enhancing the user experience. However, it's important to use them effectively, design them well and to test them before launching. By following these best practices, you can create microinteractions that are intuitive, engaging, and add value to the content. Remember, the key is to keep it simple, test it, and make sure it's consistent with the overall design of the content.

Chapter 7: microinteractions in E-commerce.

How microinteractions can enhance the user experience in e-commerce websites and apps.

In e-commerce websites and apps, microinteractions play a crucial role in enhancing the user experience. They are subtle design elements that help users accomplish tasks and interact with digital products in an intuitive and efficient way. In this chapter, we'll explore how microinteractions can be used to improve the user experience in e-commerce and provide some best practices for designing them.

One way microinteractions can enhance the user experience in e-commerce is by providing clear feedback to users. For example, when a user adds an item to their shopping cart, a micro interaction can be used to visually confirm that the item has been added and show the updated cart total. This helps users understand that their action has been completed successfully and gives them a sense of control over their shopping experience.

Another way microinteractions can enhance the user experience in e-commerce is by making it easier for users to find and compare products. For example, a micro interaction can be used to reveal more information about a product when the user hovers over it or clicks on it. This can include details such as price, size, and availability, which can help users make more informed decisions about what to purchase.

Microinteractions can also be used to improve the checkout process in e-commerce. For example, a micro interaction can be used to reveal the total cost of a user's order as they add items to their cart, helping them keep track of their spending. Additionally, microinteractions can be used to make the checkout process more streamlined and efficient, such as by providing users with a progress bar that shows the progress of their order.

One key area where microinteractions can enhance the user experience in e-commerce is through the use of animations and transitions. These can be used to make the process of browsing and purchasing products more visually engaging and fun. For example, an animation can be used to show a product being added to a shopping cart, giving the user a sense of instant gratification. Or a transition can be used to show how a product can be used or worn, giving users a better sense of what they are buying.

Another important aspect of microinteractions in e-commerce is personalization. Microinteractions can be used to create a more personalized experience for users by providing them with relevant information and options based on their browsing history or purchase history. For example, if a user frequently purchases items from a certain category, a micro interaction can be used to highlight similar products or related categories to them. This can save the user time and make it more likely that they'll find something they're interested in.

Another example of personalization is to use microinteractions to display a personalized welcome message or offer to returning customers. This can create a sense of familiarity and customer loyalty, increasing the chances of repeat purchases.

Microinteractions can also be used to improve the search functionality of an e-commerce website or app. For example, a micro interaction can be used to display search results as the user types, making it easier for them to find the products they're looking for. Additionally, microinteractions can be used to highlight spelling mistakes or suggest alternative search terms if the user's initial search returns no results.

Additionally, microinteractions can be used to improve the customer service experience in e-commerce. For example, a micro interaction can be used to provide users with quick access to customer service contact information or frequently asked questions. This can help users to quickly find the information they need, reducing the need to contact customer service and increasing customer satisfaction.

Microinteractions play a crucial role in enhancing the user experience in e-commerce websites and apps. They can be used to provide clear feedback, make it easier to find and compare products, improve the checkout process, make browsing and purchasing more visually engaging and fun, help users stay engaged with the e-commerce website or app, create a more personalized experience, improve search functionality, and improve customer service. By keeping these best practices in mind when designing microinteractions for e-commerce, designers can create a more intuitive and enjoyable shopping experience for users.

Examples of microinteractions used in e-commerce design.

In e-commerce design, microinteractions play a crucial role in enhancing the user experience and making the process of buying products or services more seamless and enjoyable. These small but powerful interactions can be used in various parts of an e-commerce website or app, from browsing products to completing a purchase.

One common use of microinteractions in e-commerce is in product listings. When a user hovers over a product image, a micro interaction can be used to display additional information such as the product name, price, and a short description. This small interaction allows the user to quickly and easily view important information without having to click on the product and navigate to a separate page.

Another example of microinteractions in e-commerce can be found in shopping cart functionality. When a user adds a product to their cart, a small animation can be used to indicate that the item has been successfully added. This animation can be accompanied by a subtle sound effect, providing an extra layer of feedback to the user and making the process of adding items to the cart feel more satisfying.

In addition, microinteractions can also be used in the checkout process. For example, when a user enters their shipping information, a micro interaction can be used to check that the address is valid and that all the required fields have been filled in. This can be done by using an animation, such as a green checkmark, to indicate that the information is correct, or by using a red exclamation mark to indicate an error. This helps to reduce the number of errors made by the user, and makes the checkout process more efficient.

Another example of microinteractions in e-commerce can be found in the product page. Many e-commerce websites use a zoom-in feature when a user hovers over a product image, allowing them to see the product in more detail. This small interaction can be accompanied by a subtle sound effect, making the experience more enjoyable and interactive.

Microinteractions can also be used to enhance the search functionality of an e-commerce website or app. When a user begins typing in a search query, microinteractions can be used to show suggested search terms or products in real-time. This can be done by using an animation, such as a sliding effect, to reveal the suggested search terms or products. This can help users find what they are looking for more quickly and easily.

Another example of microinteractions in e-commerce can be found in the wishlist feature. Many e-commerce websites allow users to save their favourite products to a wishlist for future reference. When a user adds a product to their wishlist, a micro interaction can be used to indicate that the item has been successfully added. This can be done by using an animation, such as a heart icon turning red, to indicate that the item has been added to the wishlist. This small interaction provides immediate feedback to the user, letting them know that the product has been saved to their wishlist.

Another way microinteractions can be used in e-commerce is through the use of product ratings and reviews. When a user clicks on a product rating, a micro interaction can be used to display a pop-up window with the product reviews. This small interaction allows the user to quickly view the reviews without having to navigate to a separate page. Additionally, microinteractions can also be used to indicate the average rating of a product, such as using a series of stars to display the rating, which can help users quickly identify the most popular products.

Microinteractions can also be used in the process of filtering products. When a user selects a filter, a micro interaction can be used to indicate that the filter has been applied. This can be done by using an animation, such as a checkmark appearing next to the filter, to indicate that it has been selected. This small interaction provides immediate feedback to the user, letting them know that their selection has been applied and the products have been filtered accordingly.

Finally, microinteractions can also be used in the process of making a purchase. When a user clicks on the "buy" button, a micro interaction can be used to indicate that the purchase is being processed. This can be done by using an animation, such as a loading spinner, to indicate that the purchase is being processed. This small interaction provides feedback to the user, letting them know that their purchase is being processed and that they should wait for the next step.

Microinteractions play a crucial role in enhancing the user experience of e-commerce websites and apps. They can be used in various parts of the buying process, from browsing products to completing a purchase. Examples include displaying additional information when hovering over a product image, adding a product to the cart, validating shipping information, zoom-in feature on product images, real-time search suggestions, back to top button, wishlist feature, product ratings and reviews, filtering products, and indicating the purchase process. These small but powerful interactions can make the process of buying products or services more seamless and enjoyable, resulting in increased user satisfaction and conversion rates.

Best practices for designing microinteractions in e-commerce.

Designing effective microinteractions in e-commerce can greatly enhance the user experience and increase conversions. Here are some best practices for designing microinteractions in e-commerce:

1. Keep it simple: Microinteractions should be simple and easy to understand. Complex interactions can be confusing and frustrating for users. Stick to one primary action per interaction and make sure it is clearly labelled.

2. Provide feedback: Microinteractions should provide immediate feedback to the user, letting them know the outcome of their action. This can be done through visual cues, such as changing the colour or shape of a button, or through text, such as displaying a message or confirmation.

3. Make them discoverable: Microinteractions should be easy to find and use. This means placing them in logical and intuitive locations, such as next to the action they relate to. It also means making sure they are clearly labelled and have a consistent design.

4. Make them consistent: Microinteractions should have a consistent design across the e-commerce platform. This means using the same visual cues, labels, and placement for similar interactions throughout the site. This will help users learn how to use the interactions and make them feel more comfortable using the site.

5. Use animations: Animations can add a touch of delight to microinteractions, making them more engaging and memorable for users. However, it is important to use animations sparingly and make sure they are subtle and do not distract from the primary action.

6. Test and iterate: Microinteractions should be tested with real users to ensure they are effective and easy to use. Feedback from users can be used to make improvements and iterate on the design.

7. Make them accessible: Microinteractions should be accessible to users with disabilities. This means providing alternative methods of interaction, such as keyboard shortcuts, and making sure the interactions are compatible with assistive technologies.

8. Take into account the context: Microinteractions should take into account the context in which they are used. For example, a micro interaction on a product page should be different from one on the checkout page. This will help ensure the interactions are relevant and useful for the user.

9. Use them to guide the user: Microinteractions can be used to guide the user through the e-commerce platform, helping them find what they are looking for and complete actions. For example, you can use microinteractions to highlight the next step in the checkout process or to suggest related products.

10. Consider mobile: Microinteractions should be designed with mobile devices in mind. This means using touch-friendly designs, such as larger buttons, and making sure the interactions are easy to use on smaller screens.

By following these best practices, you can design microinteractions that are simple, effective, and enjoyable for users. Remember to keep testing and iterating to ensure the microinteractions meet the needs and expectations of your users.

Chapter 8: microinteractions in Mobile.

Unique considerations for designing microinteractions in mobile apps.

Designing microinteractions for mobile apps requires unique considerations that are different from designing for web or desktop applications. In this chapter, we will explore the specific challenges and opportunities that come with designing microinteractions for mobile and provide some best practices for creating effective microinteractions on mobile devices.

One of the main challenges of designing microinteractions for mobile is the limited screen real estate. Mobile screens are smaller than desktop screens, which means that designers have less space to work with when creating microinteractions. This means that designers need to be more creative and efficient with their use of space, ensuring that microinteractions are clear, concise and easy to understand.

Another challenge is the limited input options available on mobile devices. Unlike desktop computers that have a keyboard and mouse, mobile devices typically only have a touch screen. This means that designers need to think carefully about how users will interact with the microinteraction and ensure that it is intuitive and easy to use.

The limited screen real estate and input options also mean that designers need to pay extra attention to the user experience when designing microinteractions for mobile. The microinteraction should be easy to discover, use, and understand. It should also be consistent with the overall design of the app and should not disrupt the flow of the user experience.

In addition to these challenges, there are also several unique opportunities that come with designing microinteractions for mobile. One of these is the ability to use the device's sensors and features to create more immersive and engaging microinteractions. For example, a weather app could use the device's GPS to provide a more accurate location-based forecast, or a fitness app could use the device's accelerometer to track the user's movement.

Another opportunity is the ability to use push notifications to create microinteractions that can engage users even when they are not actively using the app. For example, a social media app could send a notification to the user when a friend has liked one of their posts, or a news app could send a notification when a breaking news story is published.

Designing microinteractions for mobile requires unique considerations that are different from designing for web or desktop applications. The limited screen real estate and input options mean that designers need to be more creative and efficient with their use of space. They also need to pay extra attention to the user experience to ensure that the microinteraction is easy to discover, use and understand. However, designing for mobile also opens up opportunities for more immersive and engaging microinteractions using device's sensors and features and push notifications.

Examples of microinteractions used in mobile design.

In mobile design, microinteractions play a crucial role in enhancing the user experience. They are small animations, sounds, or visual cues that provide feedback to the user, indicating that an action has been performed or providing additional information.

One example of a micro interaction in mobile design is the pull-to-refresh gesture. This gesture allows users to refresh content on their screens by pulling down on the screen and releasing. The micro interaction here is the animation of the refresh icon spinning and the content updating once the gesture is completed. This simple interaction provides feedback to the user that their action of refreshing the content has been successful.

Another example is the use of microinteractions in push notifications. When a user receives a push notification, a small animation or sound can be used to indicate that a new notification has been received. This can be a subtle vibration or a small animation, such as a notification dot appearing on the app icon. This micro interaction provides feedback to the user that they have received a new notification without the need for them to open the app and check.

Microinteractions are also commonly used in mobile e-commerce apps. For example, when a user adds an item to their shopping cart, a small animation can be used to indicate that the item has been successfully added. This can be a simple animation such as the item bouncing into the cart icon. This micro interaction provides feedback to the user that their action has been completed and the item has been added to their cart.

In mobile games, microinteractions play an important role in providing feedback to the user and immersing them in the game. For example, when a user completes a level, a small animation can be used to indicate their success, such as confetti falling from the top of the screen. Additionally, microinteractions can be used to indicate when a user has earned a new achievement or unlocked a new feature. This can be a small animation, such as a notification popping up on the screen, or a sound effect indicating that the user has achieved something new.

Microinteractions are also used in mobile navigation. For example, when a user taps on a menu button, a small animation can be used to indicate that the menu has been opened. This can be a simple animation such as the menu sliding out from the side of the screen. This micro interaction provides feedback to the user that their action has been completed and the menu is now open.

Another important aspect of mobile design where microinteractions are used is in the process of making a purchase. For example, when a user enters their credit card information and clicks on the "Submit" button, a micro interaction can be used to indicate that the information is being processed. This can be a simple animation such as a spinning wheel or a progress bar. This micro interaction provides feedback to the user that their action is being processed and they do not need to click the button again.

Microinteractions are also used in mobile apps to indicate when a task is completed or when an error has occurred. For example, when a user submits a form and the information is successfully sent, a micro interaction can be used to indicate that the task is complete. This can be a simple animation such as a checkmark appearing on the screen. On the other hand, if an error occurs and the form cannot be submitted, a micro interaction can be used to indicate that an error has occurred. This can be a simple animation such as a red exclamation mark appearing on the screen.

Another example of microinteractions in mobile design is in the use of chatbots. When a user interacts with a chatbot, microinteractions can be used to indicate when the chatbot is typing and when a response has been received. This can be a simple animation such as a typing indicator or a sound effect indicating that a response has been received. This micro interaction provides feedback to the user that their message has been received and a response is on the way.

In addition to the examples mentioned above, microinteractions can also be used in other areas of mobile design such as image galleries, video playback, and more. The key is to use microinteractions in a way that enhances the user experience and provides feedback to the user in a clear and intuitive way.

Microinteractions play a vital role in mobile design, providing feedback and enhancing the user experience. They can be simple animations, sounds, or visual cues that indicate that an action has been performed or providing additional information. Examples of microinteractions in mobile design include pull-to-refresh gestures, push notifications, e-commerce, mobile games, navigation, making a purchase, error handling, chatbots, and more. These small details can make a big difference in how users perceive and interact with your mobile app. Designers should use them strategically and test them before release to ensure that the microinteractions are clear, intuitive and providing the feedback that users expect.

Best practices for designing microinteractions for mobile devices.

When designing microinteractions for mobile devices, there are a few key best practices to keep in mind. These best practices will help ensure that your microinteractions are effective, intuitive, and easy to use for your users.

First and foremost, it's important to keep in mind the limited screen real estate of mobile devices. Mobile screens are typically smaller than those of desktop or laptop computers, so it's essential to keep your microinteractions simple and easy to understand. Avoid using complex animations or graphics that may be hard to see or understand on a small screen. Instead, use simple, clear icons or graphics that are easy to see and understand at a glance.

Another important consideration when designing microinteractions for mobile devices is the use of touch input. Mobile devices are typically controlled by touch, rather than a mouse or keyboard. This means that your microinteractions should be designed to be easy to use with touch. Avoid using small buttons or controls that may be difficult to tap or swipe on a small screen. Instead, use larger buttons or controls that are easy to tap or swipe.

It's also important to consider the context of use when designing microinteractions for mobile devices. Mobile devices are often used on the go, in a variety of different settings and environments. This means that your microinteractions should be designed to be easy to use in different lighting conditions, and with different levels of noise and distraction. For example, if your app is used in a noisy or busy environment, consider using larger, more visible buttons or controls.

Another important aspect of designing microinteractions for mobile devices is keeping them consistent with your app's overall design. It's important to ensure that your microinteractions are consistent with the overall look and feel of your app, so that users can easily understand how to use them. This means that your microinteractions should use similar colours, fonts, and graphics to the rest of your app, so that they feel like an extension of the app, rather than a separate, disconnected feature.

It is also crucial to test your microinteractions with real users. User testing is a great way to ensure that your microinteractions are easy to use and understand. You can do this by recruiting a small group of users to test your app, and asking them to complete a set of tasks using your microinteractions. This will give you valuable feedback on what works well and what doesn't, so that you can make any necessary changes before releasing your app to the public.

Another important aspect of designing microinteractions for mobile devices is the use of gestures. Gestures are an intuitive and natural way for users to interact with mobile apps, and they can be used to create a more engaging and interactive experience. For example, a simple swipe or pinch gesture can be used to scroll through a list of items, or to zoom in on a photo. When designing gestures, it's important to keep them simple and easy to understand, and to provide clear visual feedback to indicate when a gesture has been recognized.

It's also important to consider the platform-specific guidelines when designing microinteractions for mobile devices. Different platforms, such as iOS and Android, have their own guidelines for designing microinteractions. For example, iOS has a set of guidelines for designing icons, buttons, and other controls, while Android has a set of guidelines for designing notifications and other system-level elements. By following these guidelines, you can ensure that your microinteractions are consistent with the platform, and that they feel natural and intuitive to users.

Another key aspect of designing microinteractions for mobile devices is the use of animation. Animation can be used to create a more engaging and interactive experience, and to provide visual feedback to users. For example, a simple animation can be used to indicate that a button has been pressed, or to show the results of a search. When designing animations, it's important to keep them simple and easy to understand, and to ensure that they are smooth and responsive.

Finally, it's important to keep in mind the performance of your microinteractions when designing for mobile devices. Mobile devices have limited processing power, and it's important to ensure that your microinteractions are optimized for performance. This means keeping the number of elements on the screen to a minimum, and using lightweight animations and graphics. By keeping the performance in mind, you can ensure that your microinteractions are fast and responsive, and that they don't slow down the app or drain the device's battery.

Designing microinteractions for mobile devices is an important aspect of creating an intuitive and user-friendly mobile app. By keeping in mind the limited screen real estate, touch input, context of use, consistency with overall app design, testing with real users, and being up-to-date on new technologies and design trends, as well as using gestures, platform-specific guidelines, animation and performance, you can create effective and engaging microinteractions that will enhance the user experience of your mobile app.

Chapter 9: microinteractions in Virtual Reality.

The role of microinteractions in virtual reality experiences.

The role of microinteractions in virtual reality (VR) experiences is crucial in creating immersive and engaging user experiences. Microinteractions are small, subtle animations and interactions that help to guide the user through the VR environment and provide feedback on their actions.

One key role of microinteractions in VR is in providing spatial context and orientation. For example, when a user turns their head in a VR experience, small animations such as a subtle shift in the background or a change in the position of an object can help to indicate that the user is moving within the virtual space. This can help to create a sense of presence and immersion within the VR environment, making it feel more realistic and natural.

Another important role of microinteractions in VR is in providing feedback on user actions. For example, when a user reaches out to grab an object in a VR experience, a small animation of the object being picked up or a sound effect can provide feedback that the action was successful. This can help to create a sense of physicality and interaction within the virtual environment, making it feel more responsive and engaging.

Microinteractions in VR can also be used to create a sense of progression and movement through the virtual space. For example, when a user reaches the end of a virtual pathway, a subtle animation or sound effect can indicate that they have reached a new area. This can help to guide the user through the VR experience and make it feel more cohesive and structured.

Additionally, microinteractions in VR can also be used to create a sense of atmosphere and ambiance within the virtual environment. For example, subtle animations of virtual wildlife or sound effects of a virtual forest can help to create a sense of realism and immersion within a nature-based VR experience.

It's also important to mention that microinteractions in VR have to be designed with care, as they can also cause negative effects if not well thought out. One example is the simulation sickness, a condition that can occur when the VR environment doesn't match the user's physical movements, which can cause discomfort and disorientation. Therefore, it's crucial to test and iterate microinteractions in VR to ensure they are not causing negative effects and are providing a comfortable and seamless experience for the user.

Another aspect to consider when designing microinteractions in VR is accessibility. Microinteractions can be used to provide alternative forms of interaction for users with disabilities. For example, using haptic feedback or audio cues instead of visual cues can make the VR experience more accessible to users with visual impairments. Microinteractions can also be used to provide a more inclusive experience for users with different abilities or needs. For example, providing different levels of interactivity or customizable settings can make the VR experience more inclusive for users with different levels of mobility or dexterity.

Another important aspect of microinteractions in VR is scalability. As VR technology continues to evolve and more users adopt VR devices, it's important to design microinteractions that can adapt to different hardware and software capabilities. This may include designing microinteractions that are optimized for different frame rates or resolution, or designing microinteractions that can be turned off or adjusted for users with lower-end devices.

In addition, microinteractions in VR can be used to create a sense of personalization and ownership. For example, using microinteractions to allow users to customize the virtual environment, such as adjusting the lighting or color scheme, can make the VR experience feel more personalized and engaging. Microinteractions can also be used to create a sense of ownership and investment in the virtual environment. For example, using microinteractions to allow users to interact with and manipulate virtual objects can make the VR experience feel more tangible and real.

Finally, microinteractions in VR can also be used to create a sense of community and social interaction. For example, using microinteractions to allow users to communicate and interact with other users within the virtual environment can make the VR experience feel more social and engaging. Microinteractions can also be used to create a sense of shared experience and collaboration, such as using microinteractions to allow users to work together on virtual projects or activities.

Microinteractions are a key element in creating immersive and engaging virtual reality experiences. They can provide spatial context and orientation, feedback on user actions, progression and movement through the virtual space, atmosphere and ambiance within the virtual environment, accessibility, scalability, personalization and ownership, and community and social interaction. It's important to design and test microinteractions carefully to ensure they enhance the user experience and don't cause negative effects. Additionally, considering scalability, accessibility and social interaction when designing microinteractions can make your VR experience more inclusive and enjoyable for a wider audience.

Examples of microinteractions used in VR design.

Virtual reality (VR) technology is becoming increasingly popular, with a wide range of applications in gaming, entertainment, and even education and training. As VR experiences become more immersive and realistic, it's important to pay attention to the microinteractions that help guide users through the virtual environment.

Examples of microinteractions used in VR design include:

Teleportation: A common way to move around large virtual environments is to use teleportation, where users select a location to instantly transport to. This can be done through a variety of methods, such as pointing and clicking or using a joystick or controller. This type of micro interaction helps the user to easily navigate the virtual space without becoming disoriented.

Object interaction: When users are able to pick up, move, and manipulate objects within the virtual environment, it creates a more realistic and engaging experience. Microinteractions, such as using hand gestures or controllers to grab and move objects, can make it easy for users to interact with their surroundings.

Menus and interfaces: VR experiences often have menus or interfaces that allow users to access different features or options. Microinteractions, such as voice commands or hand gestures, can be used to navigate these menus and interfaces in a natural and intuitive way.

Social interactions: VR experiences can be more immersive when they allow users to interact with other people in the virtual environment. Microinteractions, such as hand gestures or facial expressions, can be used to communicate with other users in a natural and intuitive way.

Environmental changes: Microinteractions can be used to control the virtual environment, such as changing the time of day, weather conditions, or lighting. This can help to create a more dynamic and realistic experience for the user.

Audio cues: Audio cues can be used to provide feedback or guidance to the user, such as a sound effect when the user picks up an object or a voiceover providing instructions. This can help to make the experience more engaging and immersive.

Haptic feedback: Haptic feedback can be used to provide a sense of touch to the user, such as vibrations or resistance when the user grabs an object or collides with an obstacle. This can help to make the experience more realistic and engaging.

it's important to remember that microinteractions should be designed to be intuitive and natural for the user. This means that they should be easy to understand and use, and should not be overwhelming or confusing. It's also important to test and iterate microinteractions, to ensure they are effective and enjoyable for the user.

It's also important to note that microinteractions in VR can vary depending on the type of VR experience. For example, in a gaming experience, microinteractions may focus more on object interaction and environmental changes, whereas in a training or educational experience, microinteractions may focus more on navigation and feedback.

Another important consideration for microinteractions in VR is accessibility. As VR technology becomes more widely available, it's important to ensure that the microinteractions are inclusive and accessible for users of all abilities. This can include providing options for users with visual or auditory impairments, or using alternative input methods for users with mobility impairments.

Microinteractions in VR play a crucial role in creating an immersive and engaging experience for users. By understanding the different types of microinteractions and how they can be used, designers can create VR experiences that are intuitive, natural, and accessible for all users.

In the next chapter, we will discuss the conclusion of our book. We will discuss the future of microinteractions in UX design, the importance of testing and iterating microinteractions, and resources for further learning and staying up-to-date on microinteractions in UX design. We will also summarize all key points discussed in the previous chapters and give our final thoughts on the topic of microinteractions in UX design.

Chapter 10: Conclusion.

The future of microinteractions in UX design.

The future of microinteractions in UX design is an exciting topic to explore. Microinteractions are small, subtle interactions that occur in digital products. They can be as simple as a button press or as complex as a multi-step process. They are designed to enhance the user experience by providing feedback, guidance, and convenience.

As technology continues to advance, the use of microinteractions will become even more prevalent in UX design. With the increasing popularity of the Internet of Things (IoT) and the rise of artificial intelligence (AI), the number of digital products that will incorporate microinteractions will increase dramatically.

One area where microinteractions will play a key role is in the IoT. IoT devices will be able to communicate with each other and with users through microinteractions. For example, imagine a smart home where all of the lights, thermostat, and security system can be controlled through one simple interface. Microinteractions will be used to provide feedback on the status of each device and to make it easy for the user to control them.

Another area where microinteractions will be important is in the use of AI. As AI becomes more prevalent, microinteractions will be used to communicate with users and provide them with information and guidance. For example, imagine a virtual assistant that can be controlled through voice commands. Microinteractions will be used to provide feedback on the status of the assistant and to make it easy for the user to interact with it.

In the future, microinteractions will also play a key role in the design of virtual and augmented reality (VR and AR) products. As these technologies become more advanced, microinteractions will be used to provide users with feedback and guidance in the virtual environment. For example, imagine a VR game where the player can interact with objects in the game through microinteractions.

Another important aspect of microinteractions in the future is the use of animation. Animation can be used to make microinteractions more engaging and fun. For example, imagine a button that changes colour and shape when it is pressed. This simple animation adds an element of fun and excitement to the interaction.

Microinteractions will also be used to make products more accessible to users with disabilities. For example, imagine a website that uses microinteractions to provide feedback to users who are visually impaired. This could include audio feedback or the use of haptic feedback to indicate when a button has been pressed.

important trend for microinteractions in the future is the use of natural language processing (NLP). As NLP technology continues to improve, microinteractions will be used to make digital products more conversational and intuitive. For example, imagine a chatbot that can understand and respond to user input in a natural and human-like way. Microinteractions will be used to provide feedback on the chatbot's understanding and to make it easy for the user to interact with it.

In addition, microinteractions will also play a key role in the design of smart products. These products will be able to learn and adapt to the user's preferences over time. For example, imagine a smartwatch that can track the user's exercise habits and adjust the workout plan accordingly. Microinteractions will be used to provide feedback on the user's progress and to make it easy for the user to adjust the workout plan.

Another trend for microinteractions in the future is the use of machine learning (ML) and big data. As these technologies become more advanced, microinteractions will be used to make digital products more personalized and adaptive to the user's needs. For example, imagine a music streaming app that can learn the user's preferences and create a personalized playlist. Microinteractions will be used to provide feedback on the user's preferences and to make it easy for the user to adjust the playlist.

Lastly, microinteractions will also play a key role in the design of 5G-enabled products. With 5G, devices will be able to communicate with each other at much faster speeds, which will enable new and more complex microinteractions. For example, imagine a multiplayer game that is played in real-time across multiple devices. Microinteractions will be used to provide feedback on the status of the game and to make it easy for the players to interact with each other.

In conclusion, microinteractions are an essential part of UX design and will continue to play a crucial role in the future. As technology continues to advance, microinteractions will become even more prevalent in digital products. Trends such as IoT, AI, VR, AR, animation, accessibility, NLP, smart products, ML, big data and 5G, will all impact microinteractions in the future. Designers need to stay up-to-date with these trends and technologies to design better microinteractions that will delight and engage users.

The importance of testing and iterating microinteractions.

Testing and iterating microinteractions is essential in ensuring that they are effective and user-friendly. Without proper testing, microinteractions may not function as intended or may not provide the desired user experience. Additionally, testing allows designers to gather valuable feedback from users and make necessary improvements to the microinteractions.

One of the primary reasons why testing microinteractions is important is that it allows designers to identify and fix any functional issues. For example, if a micro interaction is not working as intended, such as a button not responding when clicked, testing will reveal this issue and the designer can then make the necessary adjustments. Additionally, testing can reveal usability issues, such as a micro interaction that is confusing for users or difficult to use. By identifying and fixing these issues, designers can ensure that the microinteractions are functioning properly and are easy for users to understand and use.

Another important aspect of testing microinteractions is that it allows designers to gather valuable feedback from users. This feedback can be used to make improvements to the microinteractions and ensure that they meet the needs and preferences of the target audience. For example, if users find a micro interaction to be confusing, designers can make changes to make it more intuitive. Additionally, users may have suggestions for new features or improvements that designers can implement. By gathering feedback from users, designers can create microinteractions that are tailored to the specific needs and preferences of the target audience.

Testing microinteractions also allows designers to identify any performance issues. When microinteractions are not optimized, it can lead to slow loading times and poor performance, which can negatively impact the user experience. By testing microinteractions, designers can identify any performance issues and make necessary adjustments to improve the performance.

Another benefit of testing and iterating microinteractions is that it allows designers to continually improve the overall user experience. As users interact with digital products, designers can gather data and insights on how users are interacting with the microinteractions. This data can be used to identify areas for improvement and make adjustments to enhance the user experience. Additionally, testing and iterating microinteractions allows designers to stay up-to-date with user needs and preferences, as well as emerging trends in design and technology.

It's also worth noting that testing and iterating microinteractions is not a one-time process. It's an ongoing process that should be incorporated into the design process from the beginning and throughout the development phase. This ensures that any issues or concerns are addressed in a timely manner and that the final product is the best it can be.

When testing microinteractions, it's important to use a variety of methods to gather data and feedback. This can include user testing, where designers observe users interacting with the microinteractions and gather feedback on usability, performance and accessibility. A/B testing can also be used to compare different versions of a micro interaction and determine which one is most effective. Additionally, designers can gather data on how users are interacting with microinteractions through analytics and user feedback.

In conclusion, testing and iterating microinteractions is a crucial step in creating digital products that provide a seamless and satisfying user experience. It allows designers to identify and fix any functional issues, gather valuable feedback from users, improve performance and guarantee accessibility for all users. By testing and iterating microinteractions, designers can create digital products that are tailored to the specific needs and preferences of the target audience and stay up-to-date with user needs and preferences, as well as emerging trends in design and technology.

Resources for further learning and staying up-to-date on microinteractions in UX design.

In the final chapter of our book, "UX Microinteractions," we want to provide our readers with a variety of resources for continuing their education and staying up-to-date on the latest trends and best practices in microinteractions design. We'll be covering a range of different types of resources, including books, blogs, podcasts, and online courses, so that there's something for everyone regardless of their preferred learning style.

One of the best places to start when it comes to learning more about microinteractions is by reading books on the topic. There are a number of great books available that cover the subject in depth, including Dan Saffer's "Microinteractions: Designing with Details" and Stephen Anderson's "Seductive Interaction Design." Both of these books provide detailed explanations of the concepts behind microinteractions and offer practical tips and techniques for designing effective microinteractions.

Another great way to stay informed about the latest developments in microinteractions design is by following industry blogs. There are a number of blogs out there that are dedicated to discussing the latest trends and best practices in microinteractions design, such as the Microinteraction blog, and the Microinteraction Lab blog. By following these blogs, you'll be able to stay up-to-date on the latest research and case studies in the field.

Podcasts are also a great way to learn about microinteractions and stay current with the latest developments in the field. There are a number of podcasts that cover the topic of microinteractions, such as the "Design Details" podcast, which features interviews with industry experts and discussions of the latest trends and best practices in microinteractions design.

Online courses are another great resource for learning more about microinteractions. Platforms like Udemy and Coursera offer a wide range of courses on microinteractions, from beginner-friendly introductions to the subject to more advanced courses that delve into the details of designing effective microinteractions. Some courses to check out include "Microinteractions: Designing Details for Digital Products" and "Designing Microinteractions for Mobile and Web".

Finally, attending conferences and workshops is a great way to learn more about microinteractions and stay current with the latest trends and best practices. Conferences such as Interaction Design conference and UX Design conference and workshops such as Microinteraction workshops and Design Sprint workshops, provide a great opportunity to learn from industry experts, network with other professionals in the field, and stay up-to-date on the latest developments in microinteractions design.

In conclusion, there are many ways to stay informed and educated about microinteractions in UX design. From reading books, following industry blogs and podcasts, taking online courses, attending conferences and workshops, all these resources can help you stay current with the latest trends and best practices, and continue to improve your skills as a microinteractions designer.

Popular podcasts that cover topics related to user experience (UX) design:

1. "Design Better Podcast" by InVision: This podcast features interviews with design leaders and industry experts, as well as discussions on a wide range of topics related to design and UX.

2. "UX Podcast" by James Royal-Lawson and Per Axbom: This podcast covers a wide range of topics related to user experience, including design, research, and strategy.

3. "Design Details" by Bryn Jackson and Brian Lovin: This podcast features interviews with designers, developers, and industry leaders, with a focus on the details of design and how those details affect the user experience.

4. "UX Mastery" by David Travis: This podcast covers a wide range of topics related to user experience, including design, research, and strategy, as well as featuring interviews with industry experts.

5. "The UX Blog Podcast" by David Travis: This podcast focuses on the user experience, with interviews with industry experts and discussions of the latest trends and best practices.

6. "UX Radio" by James Royal-Lawson and Per Axbom: This podcast features interviews with industry experts and covers a wide range of topics related to user experience and design.

7. "UX Design" by Interaction Design Foundation: This podcast features interviews with industry experts and covers a wide

range of topics related to user experience, including design, research, and strategy.

8. "UX and Growth" by Samuel Hulick: This podcast features interviews with industry experts and covers a wide range of topics related to user experience, including design, research, and strategy.

9. "UX Insights" by Andrew Maier: This podcast covers a wide range of topics related to user experience, including design, research, and strategy, as well as featuring interviews with industry experts.

10. "The UX Team" by Jonathan Courtney: This podcast covers a wide range of topics related to user experience, including design, research, and strategy, as well as featuring interviews with industry experts and discussions of the latest trends and best practices.

Epilogue

In the Epilogue of our book, "UX Microinteractions," we reflect on the importance of microinteractions in the overall user experience. We have discussed in detail about how microinteractions can significantly improve the overall user experience, by making the interactions more seamless and intuitive, and by providing users with valuable feedback and visual cues. We've also shared examples of microinteractions in different contexts, such as mobile apps, websites, and smart devices, and discussed the best practices for designing effective microinteractions.

As we come to the end of our book, we want to remind our readers that microinteractions are a crucial aspect of user experience design, and that paying attention to the details of microinteractions can make a big difference in how users perceive and interact with our products. We hope that this book has provided our readers with a solid foundation in the principles and practices of microinteractions design, and that they will use this knowledge to create more intuitive and engaging user experiences.

We also want to remind our readers that the field of user experience design is constantly evolving, and that new technologies and trends will continue to emerge. We encourage our readers to stay up-to-date on the latest developments in microinteractions design by following industry blogs and podcasts, taking online courses, attending conferences and workshops and reading books on the subject. By staying informed and continuing to learn, our readers will be well-equipped to design microinteractions that delight and engage users.

As designers, it is important to remember that microinteractions are not just about making the product look pretty, but about improving the overall user experience. They are a tool that can be used to guide users through a process, provide feedback, and create a sense of delight and engagement.

As we have explored throughout this book, microinteractions can be found in a wide range of products and contexts, from mobile apps and websites to smart devices and even everyday objects. Understanding how to design effective microinteractions can make a significant difference in how users perceive and interact with our products.

We also want to stress the importance of testing and iteration when it comes to designing microinteractions. It is essential to get feedback from users and test the microinteractions in real-world situations to make sure they are intuitive and effective. This process can be time-consuming and requires patience, but the end result will be worth it in terms of user satisfaction and engagement.

In conclusion, microinteractions play a vital role in the overall user experience, and as designers, it is important to understand the principles and practices of designing effective microinteractions. This book has provided an overview of the key concepts and best practices in microinteractions design, and we hope that it has served as a valuable resource for our readers. We encourage our readers to continue learning and staying up-to-date on the latest developments in the field of microinteractions design, as it is a constantly evolving field. We believe that by understanding and utilizing microinteractions, our readers will be able to create more intuitive and engaging user experiences for their users.

About The Author

Wayne Hewitt is an experienced UX designer who is based in the United Kingdom.

Wayne has over two decades of experience and worked on numerous projects for some of the best-known brands in the sector, including Volvo, Polestar, Harvey Nash, and Jaguar Land Rover (JLR). He also has experience in designing AI dashboards for the education sector. Wayne's wealth of experience means that he is knowledgeable in all aspects of user interface design, from user research to design and implementation. His passion for user-centered design and his passion for intuitive user interfaces is evident in his work. He is dedicated to helping businesses to understand and harness the power and potential of AI to improve user experience.

Printed in Great Britain
by Amazon